# HELP ME, LORD

*Richard E. Lauersdorf*

Northwestern Publishing House
Milwaukee, Wisconsin

To all those
with whom I have stood
at the bedside of
loved ones

Fourth printing, 2012
Third printing, 2010
Second printing, 2004

Cover art by Gary Crabbe/Enlightened Images

Scripture is taken from the HOLY BIBLE, NEW INTERNATIONAL VERSION®. Copyright © 1973, 1978, 1984 by Biblica, Inc.™ Used by permission of Zondervan. All rights reserved worldwide.

All quoted hymns are taken from Christian Worship: A Lutheran Hymnal. © 1993 by Northwestern Publishing House.

Northwestern Publishing House
1250 N. 113th St., Milwaukee, WI 53226-3284
© 2003 by Northwestern Publishing House
www.nph.net
Published 2003
Printed in the United States of America
ISBN 978-0-8100-1556-2

# Contents

# 1

## HELP ME, LORD

Seeing Jesus, he fell at his feet and pleaded earnestly with him, "My little daughter is dying. Please come and put your hands on her so that she will be healed and live."

Mark 5:22,23 (NIV)

How anxious that father was! Though she was 12 years old, she was still his "little daughter." And now his precious child was seriously ill, even dying. But Jairus knew where to turn. To Jesus he hurried with his humble prayer, "Please come and put your hands on her. Help me, Lord," he pleaded, requesting healing for his beloved child but receiving much more. Before that fretful day was over, Jairus would embrace a daughter who was brought back from the dead, and a loving Savior, who had so wondrously shown his power over death.

The helper of the helpless—that's who Jesus is. Seldom do we feel more helpless than when a loved one is near death. Sometimes that dreaded moment comes after a long siege, at other times very suddenly. But the effect is still the same. Over us, almost drowning our souls, flood the horrible feelings of our own inabilities, the bitter taste of our frustrations, the fearful concerns for our own futures. What a mess life would become and what a failure death would be if we didn't have Jesus to turn to as Jairus did in his day.

Jesus could easily keep death at bay or bring our loved ones back from death, as he once did for Jairus' little daughter. Doesn't he teach us, though, to expect even greater help from him? Hasn't he told us that, on his eternal scales, never-ending life in a perfect heaven far outweighs our prolonged existence in a sin-flawed world? that sorrow caused by the loss of a loved one will be erased by the joy of finding each other again in heaven at his side? that the grand love which reddened Calvary's cross—to redeem us from sin and death—surely knows when and how to carry our loved ones safely home?

Yes, but we need the reminder. That's why we turn to God's Word as we do in the devotions of this little volume. We can never be reminded too often that God hears and answers when we plead, "Help me, Lord." Especially when our prayers come from the bedside of a dying loved one.

## Prayer

Lord, you know my situation. You know that my loved one is sick, even to the point of death. You know how feeble and frustrated I feel. How I need answers from you—and help to continue. Take me back to your cross, and remind me of your great love, which has freed my loved one and me from eternal death. In your love, let me find the power and peace I need in this time of trouble. Help me, Lord. Amen.

# 2

## It Can't Be True

When I was in distress, I sought the Lord; at night I stretched out untiring hands and my soul refused to be comforted.

Psalm 77:2 (NIV)

"No, no, no," Earl moaned. "It can't be true. I don't believe it." That morning his wife had left for work as usual. By midmorning she was in the hospital trauma center, struck down by a cerebral hemorrhage. The prognosis was less than poor. And Earl, shut down by the sudden shock, just couldn't believe it. Denial was his initial reaction.

Like a dentist's injection of Novocain, shock can serve a useful purpose. It can hold back the waves of pain that come from thoughts of losing a loved one. It gives us time to absorb disturbing news and to adjust our defenses for the distressing journey ahead. Whether we gather around a loved one who lingers with an illness or who was laid low by some sudden incident, we still experience denial. When the thought that a loved one is going to leave us finally penetrates, shock sets in.

The psalmist experienced denial too. His problems, though unstated, were heavy. He was in distress. His soul refused to be comforted. "It just can't be" was his reaction also. But the psalmist didn't remain in the state of shock. As in days of past distress, he sought the Lord. He folded his hands in untiring prayer. No matter how faint his prayer or how weak his pleading, he was looking in the right direction and at the right person—the Lord of mercy and love. From such a gracious God would come fitting answers and the faith to accept those answers, regardless of what they might be.

There's no easy way for us to begin the journey to eternity with a loved one. But the walk would be impossible if we didn't have the Lord of love to show us the final destination and the fail-proof way there. Jesus has written our names on the doors of our Father's house with the crimson ink of his blood. Our Savior has made himself the only way there. Because we know these things, we can begin the bereavement journey.

Help me, Lord. Only you can help me in the painful days ahead.

## Prayer

Lord, I just can't believe it. I don't want it to be true. Wrap your arms around me as I wrestle with the thought of having my dear one taken from me. Remind me of your great love in Christ Jesus, which covers even moments like this and conquers even enemies like death. Help me raise my eyes to you and look for your strength in the days ahead. Amen.

# 3

## IT'S JUST NOT FAIR

O LORD, do not rebuke me in your anger or discipline me in your wrath. Be merciful to me, LORD, for I am faint; O LORD, heal me, for my bones are in agony. My soul is in anguish. How long, O LORD, how long?

Psalm 6:1-3 (NIV)

Manuel was angry. Two months earlier he had retired. He was looking forward to the enjoyment of a leisurely future with his wife. But less than a week before they were to leave on a long-planned-for tour, Rosa suffered a massive stroke. Now his days were spent visiting a wife who couldn't respond, sitting helplessly at her bedside, fighting the anger that flickered within. "It's just not fair," he said to himself. He wouldn't say it to his pastor. He didn't want to say it to his God. But the thoughts were there.

The psalmist had the same thoughts, but he recognized them for what they were. Behind his anger he saw resentment against God's will and rebellion against God's ways. That's why he threw himself on the Lord's mercy. But that didn't change his situation, one that was so serious it pained his body and almost paralyzed his soul. Only the Lord of love and mercy could provide relief. To him the psalmist turned and waited eagerly for his response. "O LORD, how long?" he pleaded. "Help me in my distress."

The Lord knows our thoughts. He knows the fear, the frustration, yes, even the anger we feel when the prospect of losing a loved one looms before us. He also knows why we have such thoughts. He understands that this side of heaven, his children do not walk perfectly in his ways. We don't always welcome his will without reservation. So he sent his Son to cover our lapses and cancel their debts.

The Lord also wants us to trust that his love will deal fairly with his own—he can do no less. Even though we cannot see his purpose or understand his plans, we can trust his love. When we have trouble doing so, it's time to lift eyes of faith to his Son on Calvary's cross. There we are assured that he who did not spare his own Son will also, with him, give us all things.

May our Lord's love be the antidote for our anger and the armor for the difficult days ahead.

## Prayer

Lord, you know me inside and out. You know my thoughts even before I have them. Please forgive me when, in my weakness, I react against your will and resent your ways. Please hold the cross of Jesus before my eyes so that, in the days ahead, I trust the way you lead. Help me, Lord, to accept your will. For your love's sake. Amen.

# 4

## There Must Be Something I Can Do

So the sisters sent word to Jesus, "Lord, the one you love is sick."

John 11:3 (NIV)


We're used to wheeling and dealing in life. Who pays the sticker price for a new automobile or the advertised price for a new house? We are used to bargaining also for the lesser concerns in our lives. When it comes to deciding which TV channel to watch or which restaurant to eat in, we give a little and take a little.

Almost instinctively we try the same thing when a loved one is seriously ill. "Lord, you know how much I need my spouse, how much that child means to me, how treasured my parent is. Lord, can't we have a few more years together to raise the family, to enjoy the grandchildren, to do together the things we've planned? And, Lord, I'm willing to do anything in exchange. Just name what you would want and I'll try."

Is it wrong to think and talk that way? Of course not. We can tell the Lord what we would like. That's part of the privilege of being his beloved children and knowing him as a dear Father. Yet, just as trusting children leave the final decision up to their caring father, so we leave the final decision to our Lord. Telling him what we would like is not telling him what to do. That would be both foolish and presumptuous. We need to let our loving Father decide what is best for us and those around us. We can submit our requests with confidence in his love and submission to his perfect will.

With such confidence, Mary and Martha prayed for their seriously ill brother, Lazarus. Surely they wanted to keep their brother with them for a long time. Certainly they wanted Jesus to come and heal Lazarus. Yet note how they appealed to Jesus. "The one you love," they said, basing their appeal not on themselves but on Jesus' saving love for their brother. "The one you love is sick," they went on, stating the problem, not the solution. The solution they entrusted to the Savior's love, even when it led to the grave.

There is no better bargain than the eternal life Jesus has prepared for those who trust him. Life in heaven costs us nothing because it cost him everything. How long we do or don't have loved ones with us here on earth isn't really the main concern. Rather, we want to have them with us in eternity. And this is possible because of the Savior who loves us.

## Prayer

Lord, you know what I would like. How I want my loved one to remain at my side. But, Lord, even as I wrestle with my longings, help me bow to your will. Hear my prayers, and then answer them as a loving Father, who knows better than the child what is good. In the name of Jesus, your perfect gift to me, I ask this. Amen.

# 5

## DOES GOD REALLY CARE?

My tears have been my food day and night, while men say to me all day long, "Where is your God?"

Psalm 42:3 (NIV)

Does God really care? As troubles, trials, and tears rain down upon us, we read that smirking question on the faces of unbelievers around us. Does your God really care? If so, where is he? As sickness, sorrow, and stress squeeze us, we even find ourselves asking that searching question: Does our God really care? If so, why doesn't he do something?

That question surges through our minds with even more persistence as we sit helplessly at the bedside of a spouse, a child, a parent, or a loved one, and watch life ebbing away. Does God really care? Does he truly love us? If so, why is this happening? Has he forgotten us as he busily keeps the world turning on its axis and cares for its more than six billion inhabitants? Could it be that he has overlooked us? Could it be that we're too insignificant for him to bother about, too minuscule for him to wrap in his care?

Ah, Lord, you understand why I ask this question. You know what's happening to my loved one. You know how helpless and hopeless I feel. So please, show me the answer again. Take me to Calvary, where you hanged in agony because you cared. Show me how you shed your blood on that ragged cross, submitted to hell's dire punishments, and surrendered to cruel death—because you cared. Show me the love behind it all. A love that did not want me or my loved one to perish in hell but to live forever with you in the Father's house above. And then remind me that, for your followers, such a love colors all the circumstances in life, even death.

Where is my God? There on Calvary, dying that we might live forever. There at heaven's door, holding it open for my loved one. There at the Father's side, waiting even for me.

## Prayer

Lord, you know how confused I am, how torn by the troubles of my loved one. I just don't know where to turn and what to do. Please forgive me when in my weakness I wonder about your goodness, when in my need I worry about your abiding presence. Take me again and again to the cross of my Savior. Help me see how much you love me and how much you care. Let your saving love assure me of your caring love so that I can confidently lay my loved one in your arms. Amen.

# 6

## I Feel So Helpless

In my distress I called to the LORD; I cried to my God
for help. From his temple he heard my voice; my cry
came before him, into his ears.

Psalm 18:6 (NIV)

First he said nothing. Then he lashed out in anger at any-
one and anything that crossed his path. His wife, the nurses,
the whole world became his targets as his eight-year-old
daughter faded before his eyes. Gary didn't stop to analyze
his outbursts, but behind his anger was the horrible feeling
of his own helplessness. He, who was supposed to protect
his little girl, could only sit at her bedside, clenching his
fists. He, who was supposed to provide for her, could put
nothing on the table. What a horrible feeling helplessness
can be.

Helplessness is our feeling as we wait for those test
results from the lab. We can do nothing to make those
results turn out good. Helplessness, as the doctor outlines
the course to be taken. We can't make the medicine work or
the surgery turn out successfully. Helplessness, as we wait
with a loved one for the first chemotherapy treatment. Even
worse for the dreaded second, third, and fourth rounds.
Helplessness in full force, as the inevitable steadily creeps
up on our loved one. We try to be optimistic. We struggle

to hold on to hope. But inside we flounder, incapacitated by that horrible feeling we call helplessness.

Lash out in anger? That's one reaction. But after the shouting, we only feel worse, knowing we have hurt others. Better to do what King David did. In his heavy distress, emptied of his own strength and filled with his own helplessness, he "called to the LORD." He even stepped up the intensity of his prayers to the point that he "cried" to God for help, putting his impassioned heart and soul into his prayers. And he did so with confidence. He trusted that not only the doors of heaven but also the ears of his loving Lord were open to those prayers.

"Help me, Lord," is the answer for that feeling of helplessness. What we can't do, he can. What he will do, we leave up to him. All we need to know is that he is the helper of the helpless.

## Prayer

Lord, I feel so helpless. My loved one is sick, and I can't do anything about it. Help me call and even cry to you for help. Remind me again that you hear my prayers and that you will take care of my loved one. Help me trust that the future is in your caring hands and that you will never ask me to follow except where you lead. In Jesus' name. Amen.

# 7

## I Could Cry

"Blessed are those who mourn, for they will be comforted."

Matthew 5:4 (NIV)

When do we first learn not to cry? When we are little, the tears come quickly. Hurt feelings, a skinned knee, the loss of a pet open the fountains the wise Creator placed in our eyes. As we mature, somehow or other, we gain the feeling that tears are a no-no, that a stiff upper lip is preferred. Members of the "gentler sex" still know the value of tears. They use them as a safety valve for the soul. But males have a harder time letting go.

In his Sermon on the Mount, Jesus spoke of the value of tears. "Blessed are those who mourn," he said, using a word associated with lament for the dead or with severe, painful loss. God's children cry, first and foremost, because of their sins. When we realize how we have spit in God's face and stomped on his toes with our sins, tears come to the penitent sinner's eyes. "What have I done? How could I have done this?" we cry as we seek his pardon. When we see what the sin of our first parents in Eden brought into this world, we also cry. The pain and problems in our own lives, not to mention across the world, are enough to make us sob. It's especially time for tears when death casts its shadow over a loved one.

Our tears can say so much. They show that we care and that loved ones are precious and surely will be missed. Tears release our inner turmoil, giving relief to our feeling of helplessness. Tears also speak to our God, telling him, as we raise damp faces heavenward, that we look to and lean on him, the divine Comforter. Even as he wipes the tears out of our eyes here on earth, he points us to a heaven where "there will be no more death or mourning or crying or pain" (Revelation 21:4).

So go ahead and cry. Cry alone in your car or kitchen, in your bed or in front of your TV. Cry also with your loved one, wrapping arms around each other. Those tears mean something. And our God knows what to do with them.

### Prayer

Lord, you can see my tears, even when others can't. Keep them from being bitter tears wrenched out of a resentful heart. Let them be tears from a hurting heart anxious about a loved one, tears from a trusting heart seeking comfort from you. Please, in your love, dry my tears by pointing me to Jesus my Savior, who walks with us on earth and waits for us in heaven. Amen.

# 8

## I Accept

For no matter how many promises God has made, they are "Yes" in Christ.

2 Corinthians 1:20 (NIV)

There's a big difference between acceptance and resignation. Resignation means giving in and giving up. Nothing more can be done, so throw up your hands and wait for death. In essence, resignation is negative. It admits defeat.

How different acceptance is. When a loved one nears death, acceptance comes with difficulty. Sometimes it doesn't come at all, and the result is negative—bitterness and nagging resentment. It is always difficult—sometimes more, sometimes less—depending on who we are and what we believe. But when acceptance comes, it finally sets us free to deal with death and dying. In essence, acceptance is positive. It expresses hope.

I may be at any one of a number of different stations on the road to bereavement. My loved one may be just inching around the corner toward death or already halfway down the course—perhaps even close to the finish. But, sooner or later, I need to accept. Sooner or later—for my own good and even for the good of my loved one—I need to say, "Yes, Lord, I know what's coming. Yes, Lord, I'm trying to understand. Yes, Lord, I trust your promises."

That's the point, isn't it? Only a believer can speak about acceptance, for only a believer, by God's grace, knows and trusts God's promises. Those beautiful promises are so sure, so positive. "They are 'Yes' in Christ," as Paul put it. In Christ, God has promised and provided pardon for all our sins. In Christ, God has promised and put into place peace between a sinner and God. In Christ, God has promised and prepared an eternity filled only with positive joy and bliss. All this I need every day of my life. And, most certainly, on life's last day. All this God gives me in Christ.

God help me say, "I accept," not with resignation, throwing in the towel, but with humility and confidence, taking him at his word.

## Prayer

Lord, you know how much I would like to hide from the truth or to wish it away. I just have a hard time accepting what's happening to my loved one. So show me again your many promises in Christ Jesus. Remind me again what each of those promises means to me and that you have kept every one of them. Assured again of your pardon, peace, and permanent heavenly home, help me go forward in peace and confidence. Amen.

# 9

## I HAVE SO MANY QUESTIONS

My God will meet all your needs according to his glorious riches in Christ Jesus.

Philippians 4:19 (NIV)

Peering over the coffee cup in her hands, she blurted out nervously, "Pastor, I have so many questions." They had gone down to the hospital lunchroom while the nurses were working on her seriously ill husband. After a brief silence, she voiced her concerns. What would life be like without her mate? How would she manage with the children? What about the finances? How would she ever find her way through a future that was at best foggy and at worst pitch darkness?

Putting down his cup, the pastor leaned forward and quoted the words of Paul from memory. Paul was in prison facing death, and the Thessalonians were poor, barely able to put food on the table. They were in need. But the pastor spoke of the woman's needs, which were just as real as the needs of the Christians to whom Paul wrote. The pastor repeated Paul's promise about a loving God, who would supply all her needs. My God, the pastor called him, just as Paul had. From experience he knew that their loving God "meets" not all the wishes but all the needs of his children. And God would not grudgingly supply just enough to squeak by. He would supply them amply and gloriously.

How could the pastor be so sure? Could he see a part of the future the wife could not? No, but he did know the past. He knew that in Christ Jesus, God had already provided for our greatest need. Compared to pardon for sin and peace with God, our earthly needs are only so much "pocket change" for our gracious Lord. He who has given us the millions for our souls will supply also the nickels and dimes we need for daily life.

Then the pastor took out his pen and wrote the verse on a piece of paper. "Here," he said, "stick this in your pocket and pull it out when those questions arise."

Good advice. Of course, questions surface at times like this. And they probably won't stop soon either—perhaps never. But the answer is always the same: I have a God who promises to meet all my needs according to his glorious riches in Christ Jesus.

## Prayer

Lord, I have so many questions and so many concerns about the days ahead. You know them, even when I don't say them out loud. Help me trust that you have answers for those questions—that you will provide for my needs as you see fit. When my trust wavers, raise my eyes again to your Son's cross to see what your love has provided for me there. In his name I ask this. Amen.

# 10

## I'D LIKE TO KNOW

Now we see but a poor reflection as in a mirror; then
we shall see face to face. Now I know in part; then I
shall know fully, even as I am fully known.

1 Corinthians 13:12 (NIV)


"Just tell me why!" the distraught mother begged, as she
stood at the bedside of her critically injured teenage son.
Taking her hand, the pastor changed her question slightly.
"The why we know," he replied. "It's spelled with capital
letters—L-O-V-E. God has promised that his awesome love,
as shown in Christ Jesus, makes all things turn out for good
for his children. It's the what that we don't understand. So we
ask, "What is God's love bringing us with these circumstances? What good will he work for us and our loved one?"

When a plane crashes, investigators submit a report.
When death strikes unexpectedly, doctors perform an
autopsy to establish a cause of death. But God neither pub-
lishes statements nor prints reports. He knows what he's
doing, though he doesn't always tell us. He wants us to rest
our aching hearts on his promises and trust his saving love
to hold us. Sometimes he shows us rather quickly what his
love has in mind. At other times he makes us wait till the
fog lifts and the sunshine breaks through. At times he even
has us wait till eternity to have our questions answered.

As our hearts ache and our tears flow, we wish heaven would open so we could see our Savior face-to-face. As we wrestle to understand his ways, we weep and worry, finding scant answers for our questions. We think, "If only I could step before him right now and ask, 'Blessed Jesus, tell me what you have in mind. Show me what good your love is going to bring for my loved one and me.'" But we can't. So we ask our anguished questions about why and what, even as we struggle to lean on his love. And we trust that he'll understand.

He does! He who sweat drops of blood in the Garden of Gethsemane knows what anguish is. He who wept at the grave of his dear friend Lazarus knows how deep sorrow can be. He who breathed his last on a cross knows about victory over death. And that victory he has promised for our loved ones. That's what we need to know, even as we wait for the perfect understanding of the whys and the whats in heaven.

### Prayer

Lord, I'm hurting. I'm supposed to know that you are here and that you are in control. That you have our good in mind with what you allowed to happen. But it's so hard to understand, so hard to see. Please hold me with your arms of love. Speak to me again those words of your love. And then help me be satisfied until I see you face-to-face in heaven and know your ways as fully as you already know me. Amen.

# 11

## I NEED SOME LIGHT

Your word is a lamp to my feet and a light for my path.

Psalm 119:105 (NIV)

Is any darkness thicker than that in a hospital room where a loved one lies dying? Any gloom deeper than our feelings as we sit there, travel home, and come back, barely going through the motions of everyday living?

Each day Dinah waited for the pastor to step into her husband's room. He would barely greet them and sit down in the chair next to her husband's bed before she would ask, "Pastor, aren't you going to read to us?" She knew how necessary the light of God's Word was in the darkness that surrounded them. She even arranged her schedule so that she would be there when the pastor visited.

Maybe I'm not like Dinah. Perhaps I need a reminder of the light God has given for the dark path I am walking. No matter; the light still works. God's Word burns so brightly its light can pierce any darkness and penetrate any fog—even the dark shadow death casts.

Am I worried about my loved one's future? Let the light of God's Word shine. The Shepherd who bled for the sheep promises, "I give them eternal life, and they shall never perish; no one can snatch them out of my hand" (John 10:28).

Am I bone-weary, almost worn out by the effort of trying to cope with the burdens thrust upon me? Let the light of God's Word shine. He who carried my heaviest burden, the awful tonnage of my sin, promises, "Commit your way to the LORD; trust in him and he will do this" (Psalm 37:5).

Do I shudder inside when I try to peer into a future where I soon will tiptoe without my loved one? Let the light of God's Word shine. He who took his place in the manger and on the cross so I could be with him forever promises, "Never will I leave you; never will I forsake you" (Hebrews 13:5).

In the darkness of the hospital room and through the fog of a loved one's impending death, only one light can shine. Please, Lord, guide me with the light of your Word.

## Prayer

Lord, I need your light. The paths in which you are leading me are so dark, so filled with tears and trouble. Light my way with your promises so that I don't stumble or turn away from you. Let your Word shine brightly in my heart so that I place my loved one and myself into your hands for safekeeping. In Jesus' name I ask this. Amen.

# 12

## I Need to Know If He's Listening

This is the confidence we have in approaching God:
that if we ask anything according to his will, he
hears us.

1 John 5:14 (NIV)

They had just finished praying beside her husband's bed
when the question slipped out. "But how do we know that
God hears our prayer?" she asked quietly, almost apologet-
ically. The day of trouble is also the day of prayer. Sinking
times are good praying times. Peter discovered that one
stormy night on the Sea of Galilee. To pray confidently
though, we need some reminders.

I don't send my prayers to some indefinite anybody,
some indefinable "To whom it may concern." My prayers
soar heavenward to God. Who and what this God is, the
Bible has clearly told me. He is my loving Father through
Christ Jesus. When I stand before him with my fervent
petitions, he doesn't see me, the sinner; rather, he sees me,
the saint, covered with the holy, precious blood of his Son.
He reaches out his arms to me, his own dear child, and
encourages me as he lifts me up on his lap, "It's okay, tell
me all about it." Oh, how I need to know this as my
prayers rise almost constantly in my current hour of need!

Without the assurance of a loving Father's open ear, my prayers can only stick in my throat.

Nor do I send my prayers to some caring, but not always capable, listener. Unlike earthly fathers who want to do what is best but don't always know what the best is, who want to help but aren't always capable, my Father in heaven always knows and always helps. From him I can expect only right answers, given always in ways that are wise. He's not some ATM machine into which I insert a card to obtain what I want. He knows what I need even before I ask, and he delivers accurately and on time.

So should I pray that God restore my loved one to health or extend the days a bit longer? Or should I ask that he take my dear one soon and end this time of turmoil? Can I tell him about my own anxious thoughts and expect him to understand? Of course! On my Father's loving lap, I can open my heart. As I do, I add trustingly, "according to your will." Even if I can't always find the words, he will nod his head sympathetically. Even better, he will open his caring hand and give me what he knows I really need.

Dear Father, help me pray with such confidence.

## Prayer

Lord, sometimes the words just don't seem to come. And when they do, I wonder if you're listening. Show me your love again, as it took the form of your own Son, given for me on Calvary's cross. Then help me trust that you will provide what is best for me and my loved one. Lord, help me to pray this way, always confident of your open ear and your caring answers. Amen.

# 13

## I Don't Know What to Say

A man finds joy in giving an apt reply—and how good is a timely word!

Proverbs 15:23 (NIV)

Sometimes silence is golden. Just being there, holding his hand, touching his brow, tells my loved one that I care. I don't have to talk all the time, nervously filling in the silence. My very presence speaks of my ongoing support and God's embracing love.

At other times words are very much in order. What I say and how I say it can bring much comfort. The right words to speak might be an invitation, "Tell me what you're really thinking," or similar phrases that I've used in the past to open a dialogue. My loved one needs the assurance, whether from my words or my silent presence, that my heart and ears are open. I do him a disservice if I refuse to talk about his condition or am not ready to listen when he wants to talk.

My loved one needs to hear how much he means to me and our family. We often find it difficult to express our love for one another. Sometimes now, as death draws near, it becomes even harder. Reliving pleasurable moments from the past, like the circumstances of our meeting, the silly things we did in our dating days, and the early years of our marriage, can usher a little sunshine into that sickroom. Recalling the hard times, the challenges we faced and the obstacles we scaled together, can brighten both our spirits. Relaying the concerns of the present also helps. When those getting ready to leave and those who will remain share their inner thoughts and concerns, both benefit.

What about the most precious words of all, those spoken to us by God? Speaking God's Word is not the privilege of the pastor alone. It's also mine. What more "apt reply" can I offer my loved one than the reminder that God so loved and gave his best that we might not perish but have eternal life? What more "timely" words can I speak than those about Jesus, who loves us and who, when our short lives are ended, will "fold us to his breast, there within his arms to rest"?

Lord, above all, help me speak such words to my loved one.


### Prayer

Lord, at times the words come so hard. I don't know what to say and what to do. Please unlock my ears and unloose my tongue. Help me open the door to honest conversation with my loved one, showing I'm ready to listen and respond with concern. Above all, help me share your concern with my loved one so that together we can find the comfort we need in your precious promises. Amen.

# 14

## I NEED MORE STRENGTH

[God] comforts us in all our troubles, so that we can comfort those in any trouble with the comfort we ourselves have received from God.

2 Corinthians 1:4 (NIV)

"How can they do it?" the nurse asked me. Their ten-year-old son was dying of an inherited kidney disease. Dialysis wasn't helping anymore, and the boy, who had spent more time in than out of the hospital, was living his last days. Father and mother were constantly at his bedside, comforting their child and being comforted by God's love. Others who looked in couldn't understand it. How could these parents seem to be so calm, so accepting of what appeared to be a tragedy?

When the Lord allows trouble to hit our lives, it's like tossing a pebble into a pond. Waves result. The first waves engulf the one who bears the sickness or trouble, like little Arnold in that hospital bed. The second set of waves reaches those who are close, like Arnold's parents. The outer waves extend to all those looking in, like the nurses, doctors, and extended family.

What sermons we preach in the day of trouble! The way we react on that day speaks volumes to those around us, often without our even knowing it. And we want to send the right message. We want our witness to speak of a God whose love has taken care of our souls and whom we also trust to deal lovingly with our bodies.

But that's not easy. Arnold's parents had their down times too. They regularly needed strengthening from Scripture, either from the mouth of their pastor or through their own searching. Comforted daily by God's promises, they could comfort others by their example.

Do we respond, "But I can't do that. I just can't be that strong"? Crying times are important too, so that the family members can wrap comforting arms around one another. Then, after we've felt our helplessness again, it's time for reinforcement. Time for us to reach for the Word, read again of our Father's great love, and be renewed for the struggle.

## Prayer

Lord, you know how weak I am and how I'm crumbling inside. So often I'm close to tears. Draw me into your Word that I might be comforted by your divine love. Let that love relieve my tears and renew my strength so that I can face this day of trouble as your confident child. Comforted by you, help me be a source of comfort to those around me. Amen.

# 15

## We Need to Make Some Plans

By faith Joseph, when his end was near, spoke about the exodus of the Israelites from Egypt and gave instructions about his bones.

Hebrews 11:22 (NIV)

One of the last things many want to talk about with loved ones is death. For them it's a subject to slide over as speedily as possible, an event to wish out of existence as long as possible. Even when death draws near, talking about it can be difficult.

Not for Joseph. Gathering his family around him, he spoke about what should happen when he died. He even bound his brothers by oath to carry out his plans. They were to bury his body back in the land of Canaan. Though this mighty man of Egypt had spent only the first 17 years of his life in the Promised Land, his instructions about his bones revealed his faith in God's promises. His grave's location was his statement of faith. He believed that God's promise to give the land of Canaan to Abraham's seed would come true. Better still, his choice for a burial plot showed his confidence that God would send the Savior from Abraham's seed just as promised.

So it's time to make some plans, if my loved one and I haven't done so already. Time to have the necessary talks about things such as tax sheltered annuities and life insurance policies. Time to think over what to do with the house title and the car registration papers. Time to discuss wills and how to handle the present needs and how to prepare for future necessities. Talking about such things doesn't speed death's approach. It shows the practical, positive side of God's invisible gift to us—our faith in his promises.

Faith discusses even more practical plans, like the hymns and Scripture passages to be used for the funeral. Even more important, faith talks about the sure hope for heaven. Uncomfortable feelings over the discussion about burial plots begin to fade when faith's eyes see the opened graves on the day of resurrection. The conversation about funerals takes a positive perspective when it centers on the risen Savior's promise, "Because I live, you also will live" (John 14:19).

It's not easy to talk with a loved one about death, not even for Christians. But when God leads with his promises, the discussion can begin.

### Prayer

Lord, I know we have to look ahead. I don't want to, but it's time. Help me discuss with my loved one how to handle the earthly goods you have so graciously given us. Help me talk also about important subjects like funeral and burial plans. Above all, help me speak about spiritual things—about our sure hope of heaven and our future reunion at your side in heaven. In the risen Savior's name, I ask this. Amen.

# 16

## I Know Him, and He Knows Me

"I am the good shepherd; I know my sheep and my
sheep know me—just as the Father knows me and
I know the Father—and I lay down my life for
the sheep."

John 10:14,15 (NIV)

"I know how you feel." I don't know if I can bear to hear
those words one more time. Well-meaning friends want to
comfort me. They want to be there for me. They want me to
know that they feel for me. But they can't be feeling what I
am. It's not their loved one who's dying. It's mine. They
aren't walking in my shoes so how can they know what the
journey is like?

The Good Shepherd knows. "I know my sheep," he
declares, using a word that indicates experience and concern.
He doesn't just know about me; he knows me! He doesn't
just recognize me as some acquaintance; he claims me as his
very own. He doesn't just know the dates and details of my
life; he's involved in every one. So close and intimate is his
relationship with me that he compares it to the loving relationship that exists between him and his Father.

So the Shepherd can say, "I know how you feel. I feel
your pain. I understand your sorrow. I appreciate how tired
and troubled you are." And then he reaches for me. "Here,"

he says, "let me hold you like a lamb in my arm. Here, let me fold you close to my heart, which beats constantly with love for you. Here, let me carry you on the difficult path ahead. Together we can make it—you and I."

Can I trust him? The nail print in the hand that reaches for me gives the answer. The spear wound in his side where I am nestled repeats it. The Good Shepherd loves me. He already has given his best for me. He has laid down his life so that I can be his own forever.

By God's grace and the Spirit's work, I know him! Now, in my hour of need, I need to be reminded again that he knows me.

## Prayer

Lord, help me remember and receive comfort from these words I learned as a child:

> I am Jesus' little lamb;
> Ever glad at heart I am,
> For my shepherd gently guides me,
> Knows my needs and well provides me,
> Loves me ev'ry day the same,
> Even calls me by my name. Amen.

# 17

## I Don't Know What to Ask For

[Jesus] fell with his face to the ground and prayed, "My Father, if it is possible, may this cup be taken from me. Yet not as I will, but as you will."

Matthew 26:39 (NIV)

"Pastor, did I do wrong?" he asked. His once energetic, vibrant wife was in a coma, the victim of a sudden, severe stroke. The days were inching slowly by with no sign of recovery. By himself, with the pastor, and with his family that husband had prayed for his wife's recovery. But nothing was happening. The future was bleak. Finally one evening, as he sat alone with his unresponsive wife in that hospital room, he begged, "Lord, please take her home." Now he felt guilty. Should he have prayed that way?

In answer, the pastor pointed to the Savior. With his face in the dirt of that olive tree garden, feeling the overwhelming weight of the world's sins, facing not only the pains of physical death but of eternal damnation, Jesus turned to his Father. Because it was his Father, he knew he could ask. Was there some other way? Could the redemption of the world be accomplished without his needing to drain the bitter cup of hell's poison? Because he was the Father's Son, Jesus knew the Father would answer. The answer might be different from what he was asking. But it did not matter. His Father's will would be right, and he would follow it.

May I pray that the Father take my loved one home? If the thoughts filling my heart are flavored with defeat, if it's "What's the use? Let's get it over with," I might want to reconsider. If it's resentment welling up; if it's "What good does it do to pray? It won't make any difference anyway," I might want to hold back. But if it's deep concern that my dear one be spared further discomfort, that the battle might end and the victory come, I can pray as Jesus did. Though always adding as he did, "Yet not as I will, but as you will."

Even Jesus did not always get what he asked for in prayer. But there's no sin in asking when I'm willing to receive whatever answer my loving Father sends.

### Prayer

Lord, I want to pray for what is right. I want to follow your will. You know how sick my loved one is, how perilous life appears. You know also how we trust you for the heaven you have promised. So, please understand when I ask that you take my loved one home—shorten the journey through this vale of tears and give the crown of life in heaven. Yet not as I will, but as you will. Amen.

# 18

## I Want to Learn How to Sing

About midnight Paul and Silas were praying and singing hymns to God, and the other prisoners were listening to them. Suddenly there was such a violent earthquake that the foundations of the prison were shaken. At once all the prison doors flew open, and everybody's chains came loose.

Acts 16:25,26 (NIV)

The sound carried up and down the hospital corridor. Grandma's children were singing to her again. The songs they had learned on their mother's lap and the favorite hymns they had sung with her on the church bench provided the words. Though they couldn't tell whether their unconscious mother actually heard them, her lips did seem to form a smile. Many others, though, were listening.

Back in Philippi, Paul and Silas had been seized on trumped-up charges. After being stripped of their clothing and shamefully beaten, they were secured hand and foot in stocks in a locked jail cell; they could neither stand up nor sit down. How did they react? Not by moaning in pain or muttering in anger, but by making melody to the Lord at midnight! What psalm verses they used to send their prayers heavenward we aren't told. But in singing those words, they were both turning to the Lord and comforting each other.

Their songs did even more. They offered comfort to the other prisoners in the cell block who were listening.

Under the present circumstances, perhaps singing isn't the easiest thing in the world for me to do. But if I keep looking at Jesus, the notes will come, sometimes faintly, sometimes tearfully, sometimes triumphantly. Perhaps my song will not be set to music. But the words will be familiar. They will speak of the Lord who is my Shepherd, my salvation, my strength. They will recall precious redemption, promised help, the sure prospect of heaven. Perhaps my loved one can't hear all my words, but others may pick up some of them. Perhaps no hospital door will open to return my loved one to me; instead, an even greater miracle is waiting. Heaven's door stands open, ready to receive my loved one when it's time.

Lord, help me sing into the night that has fallen upon me, for the sake of myself, my loved one, and those around me.

## Prayer

Help me to sing, Lord. The words may come hard, but they need to come. Both my loved one and I need to be reminded of what you have done for us in Christ Jesus, and what you have waiting for us. We need your strength for the time ahead and your promise of the unending time of joy waiting for us in heaven. In Jesus' name. Amen.

# 19

## I'm Not Lost, Just Bewildered

But as for me, it is good to be near God. I have
made the Sovereign LORD my refuge; I will tell of all
your deeds.

Psalm 73:28 (NIV)

Someone asked Daniel Boone, late in life, if he had ever
been lost in the woods. Back from this veteran explorer,
survivor of many a wilderness exploit, came the answer,
"No, never lost, but I was bewildered once for three days."

I think I know what he meant. The woods in which I'm
walking is thicker than any virgin wilderness Boone ever
faced. Some days as I watch over my loved one, the way
seems so clear. I can feel the Savior's presence and find comfort in his promises. I can accept the end that is approaching
and be assured of the heaven to which it's leading. I may even
pray that the time come quickly for the sake of my loved one.

Then, almost before I know it, I'm bewildered. As the
forest closes in on me, it seems so dense; the way through
it, so difficult; the final destination, so distant. If only I
could have my loved one's health back. If only the Lord
would hear me. If only I could see heaven and be sure. If
only I knew what I'm going to do without my loved one.
Just like that, I seem to be going around in circles and getting nowhere.

The psalmist has words for such times. "But as for me, it is good to be near God," he reminds me. How can I be lost if the Lord is guiding? Not only has my heavenly explorer marked the trail through the woods, he now walks with me on the path. When I grow weary, I can turn to him as my refuge. The almighty Lord knows and grants what I need in order to continue on my journey. Better still, hasn't he already blazed the trail to heaven with his own death and resurrection? Hasn't he promised to be the sure guide when my loved one and I myself have to walk that trail?

When my eyes waver from him, I become bewildered. With my eyes on him, I can never be lost.


## Prayer

Lord, help me keep eyes of faith ever on you. So often I'm tempted to look at my situation, my needs, my concerns—and then I feel lost. Send your Spirit to guide me, through your Word, in this present hour. In your Word help me find the assurance that you know where you are leading me and the strength to follow your lead. In Jesus' name. Amen.

# 20

## I Need to Hear about the Giant-Killer

[Christ Jesus] has destroyed death and has brought life and immortality to light through the gospel.

2 Timothy 1:10 (NIV)

This time little Rosita's parents asked, "Tell us again about the Giant-Killer." On my first visit with their six-year-old, dying because of an inoperable heart defect, I had told them about young David's going out against the giant Goliath. The comparison was obvious. Little Rosita was going up against the Goliath named death, but, like David, she would use the Lord's strength—and win. Now that the end was near, she and her parents needed to hear again about Jesus, the Giant-Killer, in whom believers have the sure victory over death.

That victory is what our Savior brings. Paul says that Jesus "has destroyed death." The word means more than to knock death down. It means to wipe death out, utterly abolish it, render it completely ineffective. Paul also says that Jesus "has brought life and immortality to light." Instead of ugly death breathing down upon us, we now have immortal life beckoning us. Hell's shadows have been brushed aside; heaven's never-ending light breaks before us. Those whom the God of grace has brought out of unbelief's spiritual death to faith need not fear physical death.

For them it is the escalator that carries them safely to the upper floor of heaven.

How can I be so sure? As my loved one lies dying, I need to know. So I listen to Paul again. "Through the gospel," he reminds me. In the gospel, God has recorded for me the beautiful account of how his Son went up against that giant and wiped out death on Good Friday and Easter Sunday. In the gospel—just as if I were there on that first Good Friday—I hear the Savior say of sin's payment, "It is finished." In the gospel, I see the risen Jesus standing before me, just as if I had been with his disciples that first Easter. In the gospel, I find the assurance that the Father was satisfied with his payment. Through that same blessed gospel, the Spirit has opened my eyes of faith to see all this. Through that same gospel, he keeps them open.

Death is a Goliath, the biggest giant I face in life. Jesus, the crucified and risen Savior, is my David. He has not only knocked death down but wiped it out. As I sit at my loved one's bedside, please tell me again about the Giant-Killer.

## Prayer

Lord, the end is approaching. Now more than ever I need the assurance of your victory over death. Through your gospel, take me ever closer to your filled cross and emptied tomb. Assure me again that with your payment for sin, you have erased sin's debt of death. Fill my anxious heart with peace as I see you hold open the door of heaven for my loved one. For your love's sake, I ask this. Amen.

# 21

## WHAT IS DEATH LIKE?

We live by faith, not by sight. We are confident, I say, and would prefer to be away from the body and at home with the Lord.

2 Corinthians 5:7,8 (NIV)

Nobody has ever returned to tell us about death. Scripture offers no record of any conversation with Jesus' friend Lazarus, who was brought back from the dead. No commentary from Jairus' daughter or the widow of Nain's young son, though we would be interested in what they might have to say. Could it be that our Savior wants us to trust him, to "live by faith, not by sight" as life's greatest mystery draws near?

The omniscient Savior knows how many questions swirl around me at such an anxious time as this. He understands the concerns connected with my loved one's approaching death. And he has told me what I need to know. Through his apostle he describes death as being "away from the body and at home with the Lord." At that last moment my loved one's soul will leave the body. Let medical science talk about the absence of a pulse or brain waves to pinpoint the time—my Lord knows exactly. And when that moment arrives, so will his angels. Just as they carried beggar Lazarus' soul home to Abraham's bosom, so they will carry my loved one. Just as the Savior promised the penitent thief, "Today you will be with me in paradise" (Luke 23:43), so it will be for my loved one. At death's precious moment, his soul will be "at home with the Lord."

His body, the house in which his soul lived while on earth, will still lie before me. Like an abandoned building, that body will start falling apart. No matter, for again the Savior has told me what will happen. On the Last Day, he has promised that he will return and he will raise that decaying body from the resting place my love has given it. He will reunite the soul with the body, in glorified form, to be forever with the Lord.

Lord, in your Word you described faith as "being sure of what we hope for and certain of what we do not see" (Hebrews 11:1). Make this true for me, Lord, at this anxious moment. Help me walk by faith in your precious promises, till in heaven I have perfect sight.

### Prayer

Lord, I need to know what's going to happen. Even though I can't see it happen, tell me again how you will carry my loved one's soul home to heaven. Tell me again that you also will care for his body, that on the Last Day you will put it back together from the dust of the grave and unite it with his soul. Tell me again of the forever joys of heaven, prepared and paid for by your precious blood. Amen.

# 22

## I Want to Be There

The LORD replied, "My Presence will go with you, and
I will give you rest."

Exodus 33:14 (NIV)

She didn't want to miss it. She would hurry to the hospital cafeteria and hastily eat her soup and sandwich. At
night she was reluctant to head home, even though the
nurses assured her that they would call. What if she wasn't
there when her loved one breathed his last? In life they had
shared so many steps. Now she wanted to be there for his
final step.

Sometimes it works out that we can be there to whisper
our last good-bye to those we love. Sometimes it doesn't,
and we can only wish that we had been there. Whether we
can be at a loved one's deathbed or not, just think how difficult that moment would be without the Lord's promise,
once given to Moses. Facing the unknown in the wilderness, fighting a rebellious Israel, fearful that God would tire
of them and throw them aside, Moses in his extreme need
turned to the Lord. The answer he received is just what we
need for our time of extreme need.

"My Presence will go with you," the Lord promises. It's
even more reassuring in the original Hebrew. "My *face* will
go with you," he says. Day and night, minute after minute,

hour after hour, he promises to look upon his children. We know what we'll find on that divine face: love beyond degree, concern beyond description, compassion beyond comprehension. God's face smiled upon my loved one at the baptismal font, putting the sign of the Savior's cross on his chest. God's face beamed upon us together through life as we basked in the precious promises of his pardon and peace. Now God's face, with all his love, compassion, and care, will look upon my loved one at his last moment. Even though I may not be there, the Lord will.

With the Lord himself smiling upon my loved one, the result is predictable. "I will give you rest," the Lord told Moses. For my loved one, that final moment will bring rest from the painful rigors of this brief life—rest in the perfect joys of heaven. For me too there is rest; that same Lord smiles on me. And, though I will sorrow at my loss, I can still rejoice. In heaven my loved one will see the Savior face-to-face, a glorious sight for which I still have to wait.

## Prayer

Lord, you know how much I want to be there when my loved one draws his last breath. Above all, you know how much I need the assurance that you will be there, looking on him with your gracious love. Be with him; keep him safe into eternity. Be with me; comfort me with your abiding presence. In the smile of your love, both my loved one and I are safe. Amen.

# 23

## Show Me the Empty Grave

But Christ has indeed been raised from the dead, the firstfruits of those who have fallen asleep.

1 Corinthians 15:20 (NIV)

The end is near, perhaps only minutes away. The pastor has been here, offering comfort from God's Word. I can almost see heaven's doors open, waiting to welcome my loved one home. But at times tears blur my vision. At times I hear doubt's nagging voice. Death seems so final, the grave so foggy, the future so indefinite. I don't even want to put my anxious thoughts into words—but I'm thinking them. And I need reinforcement.

Paul takes me where I need to go—back to Christ's empty grave. The Savior's resurrection is the antidote for my pressing doubts, the proof positive of the believer's eternal future. If Jesus' grave still held his body, if the linen strips still covered his corpse, my tears would know no end. They would be the bitter foretaste of the ones I would have to shed in the fires of hell. And what about my loved one? His death would still be the wages of his sin. His journey could only lead to hell's dead end. And I would have nothing in which to find comfort. Dejection, defeat, and despair would be fitting words for funeral times; not victory, joy, and blessed anticipation.

But that's not how it is. Thank God, it isn't. "Christ has indeed been raised from the dead." Sin is paid for; death, defeated; heaven, opened. Now death for my loved one is an Easter day. I can help carry him to the grave because of the Savior's resurrection. As the first daffodil in spring is a promise of more to follow, so Christ's empty grave previews what is coming. Though my physical eyes see only the door on the grave labeled "entrance," faith's eye sees a second door, the one labeled "exit." And that door has already been opened wide by the Savior's resurrection.

Jesus was speaking of my loved one too when he said, "Because I live, you also will live" (John 14:19). The Savior's empty grave is the sure promise of what awaits his children.

### Prayer

Lord, show me your empty grave. Repeat for me once again the blessed truths of your resurrection. Assure me that your eternal home is waiting for my loved one. Strengthen my spirit with the reminder that when the final day comes, you will call his body out of the grave, already opened by your rising. Let these truths take the bitterness out of my tears and the doubts out of my heart. Amen.

# 24

## I Can't Wait for the Family Reunion

And so we will be with the Lord forever.

1 Thessalonians 4:17 (NIV)

Can there be a briefer, more beautiful description of heaven? Everything I need to know is condensed into these nine brief words.

"We," Paul says. Heaven will be God's family reunited—all believers back together. In this world we so often experience the opposite. Children mature and move miles away, particularly in our mobile society. At times, even when we may live near each other, internal stress pushes family members apart. Sooner or later, death barges in, claiming loved ones and creating holes in the family circle. But in heaven! What a family reunion that's going to be, with none of God's children missing.

"With the Lord," Paul continues. Won't that be the best part of heaven? In heaven we will see Jesus face-to-face. We'll delight in the full knowledge of his saving love. We'll understand clearly the ways he has led us as we journeyed through life and how straight toward heaven his ways have always pointed. We'll walk the golden streets of the new Jerusalem, singing our Redeemer's praises with Adam and Abraham, Mary and Joseph, James and John, parents and grandparents, children and other family members. What a family reunion that's going to be at the Savior's side, one I surely don't want to miss!

"Forever," Paul concludes. How different from my family on earth. Right now "forever" seems so faint. Right now, as death ends our brief earthly time together, the forever of heaven seems so far away. But, Lord, you promised. And you said that I could count on your promise. Please give eyes of faith to my loved one and me so that we don't miss heaven's never-ending family reunion.

### Prayer

Oh, sweet and blessed country,
The home of God's elect!
Oh, sweet and blessed country
That eager hearts expect!
Jesus, in mercy bring us
To that dear land of rest;
You are with God the Father
And Spirit ever blest. Amen.

# 25

## My Only Help—Jesus

Jesus said to her, "I am the resurrection and the life. He who believes in me will live, even though he dies; and whoever lives and believes in me will never die."

John 11:25,26 (NIV)

I can't see him, but he's here. He'll be at the funeral too. And how I need him! None but the Lord Jesus can offer me the help I need now. He knows how I'm feeling. He sees my tears. He even joins me in my tears. Just as he wept with Mary and Martha at the grave of their dear brother, so he weeps with me. His spirit sighs, his throat is thick, his eyes are wet as he shares the anguish my loved one's death has brought. He, who has plumbed the depths of human misery himself, now mingles his tears with mine to assure me that he cares.

He does more than care. He speaks of his power. Nothing is beyond his grasp. Nothing is too much for his strength, not even death. That was the claim he made that day to Mary and Martha. The grave had locked in their brother four days earlier, but the master declared him still alive. "He who believes in me will live, even though he dies," Jesus stated. Mary and Martha, facing the same physical death in the future, received the same promise of life eternal. "Whoever lives and believes in me will never die," their heavenly friend assured them. Jesus' words weren't meant just for the brother and those two sisters that day at Bethany. He meant them for me too, in my day, at the grave of my loved one.

Jesus did more than speak of his power over death that day. He demonstrated it! With a loud voice he called out, "Lazarus, come out!" If he hadn't named his friend, all the other graves in that cemetery would have opened too. So powerful is the Lord of life and death. Now he stands with me in the cemetery at the grave of my loved one. How I need his promise that though physical death still came to my loved one and will eventually come to me, it doesn't lead to hell's eternal death. Instead, it's the means the Prince of life uses to usher our souls to heaven, where one day he will also take our raised and renewed bodies.

What priceless comfort to know my loved one's soul is safe in Jesus' keeping! What precious assurance to look ahead and hear Jesus calling to my loved one's body, "Come out!" No one but Jesus can offer me such help!

## Prayer

Lord, be with me, especially now. Wrap your arms around me, and assure me that you weep with me. Open my heart to hear your assurance that those who believe in you are not dead but living with you. Dry my tears with this sweet comfort, and prepare my heart with your sure promise that whoever lives and believes in you will never die. Amen.